Vaudeville Jihad

Poems by Nate Maxson

Immolation in two movements

Exhalation
Springtime arrow ready sucks in air, quiver of
clarinet caterpillar sky-lust

Splinter, wounded queen of shivers exhale afraid

I said I would wait agelessly for the callused
carpenters to make something fun from historical
wreckage

Sinking rubber feeling ducky titanic regret

We never respected distances

Until they stared us wide and absurd with bright cornfield oblivion in the face

A riot of blueberries and bald eagle toupees

Coin the term frost drill bit cash register clank

Rigged to blow away the waxing moon birthday candles

Serotonin tanning bed shot stretch of ghost town nostalgia in the withered arm

Tumble weed hairbrush trying to piece together for the third time

Old yellowed photographic memory

We tried to hold onto a nostalgia that wasn't ours, didn't we?

A wineglass wise man kiss ass tongue busted

Fate is not a kidnapped light circle and I am no turning point of contention

Thrown out protesting by bankers with bootspurs

Fifteen minutes of arbitrary sound brought 30 minutes of contentment

Bitter theft leg scratching

Near death work experience head on the wall
origami folder

Astrological chalk marks on the sidewalk all wave
north

Egg filter jellyfish jetstream film trailer park

Ready to drizzle parachute pants my intensity

Speak exquisite into the executioners' armchair

It will take a special spatula to pry me off

The carbon-dating game bowtie twirl

Just be clear where you want to shove justified
distraction

When pointing the rainstick at a miraculous lizard
sunburn

Pour spackle whitewash over the desert

Banana peel clunker slip crank, sailor I am not

The oceans of your youth are sickly ragdoll puddle

Everything circling a bathtub drain I know I won't
gurgle

Ever be a champion hog-skinner

You can't justify the melting of saxophones for horseshoes nor the butchering of horses to harvest heat

Tornado fat ten by ten cell, ha ha crow cigar sweatshop pun manufacturer

Forehead jubilant slap raw mosquito of the drenched slum

I can't read your kool-aid tattoos, foreign forever no matter where

Substitute my sarcasm for a mystic hamburger

Polluting the goddess' fourth eye tied to the railroad tracks with used chewing gum

Milky marble ionic newspaper column

Mice in a castle of rats slurping the dry mouthed good stuff tried to say help

Running out of hundred degree particles from concentrate down the concrete

Down deep breath brat-syrupy dream-fluid stolen from rotten eggs who peaked early

Slow, slowed spitty movement metabolism of a gambler

Cough cog chrome rollover clock sleeper

You never were a real gleaming sharp fishhook

A chewed fingernail took all afternoon to rocket lift
off just once from the breadcrumb table

Inhalation
Unsure, perhaps even hesitant to step forward into
an obvious sinkhole

Tiptoe thickboot, tiptoe, and don't wake the
napping jackals

Entombed in that softsighted electric forest

Porous whistle termite fence, Kansas hush gold road

Trying to constitute blank-face empty reason circle

Confirm a fuzzed out remembrance blast of static
dumpster

Strange blinking appliance light of civilized plastic
rabbit feet

We buried the elephant deep with shovels made
from his bones

Wanting to stop the huffing of earthquake dust

These hills should shake their vesuvial hips for no choice but ours, right?

A stew of attempts stirred rotten but oh so ozone tasty

Pruning the tree of warm meat curiosity

Borderland between rain of night squeezed oranges

Wet and reluctant on heavy branches

Train tracks sunken in old divide the north side of town from the south

Empty space unclaimed except by locomotive crows

I have been to a white city abandoned through a contortion of time

The mumble beep warning noise right on target

Green becomes white and ash becomes green

A drop of nectar holds sweet breathlessness immaculate and jumps

Lamppost put out whooshed cyclops

Metallic reach Neptune-blue marble analysis

Crouched with tulips twisted saccharine

So sweet before the moss grew between my stone hands

The dried sunflower old seed skeletons accept my parched footsteps

But I am not the traveler for whom they unconsciously stand vigilant fearless of frost

We wait, all crunchy used up temptations bones shoving in line for circular satisfaction

Desiring quick to catch that sad thunder voice before blindness

Meteor teeth xylophone, you cannot put the sound in shackles

Butterfly net my body made of mirror shards, wind skin mesmerize

Stomp a barefoot tangle naked in the drumheart stormtap

Pulled by the grassy hair towards central water burial silence

I stand fullbellied in this cookiecrumb bedroom doorway dripping the loss of my voice

It remains either unclear or unspoken, which one of
our muddy shores sighs more impossibility

So I think I've finally gone and done it now

I watched from the curb bouncing a baseball in my
left hand

As the big men with their mermaid tattoos packed
up all the uneaten birthday cakes in black trashbags

And took them away where nobody could eat them

I wonder if there's a tropical island somewhere
being ruined because all the uneaten birthday cakes

With their melted wax and smudged happys
dumped unceremoniously SPLATT from planes into
palm trees

The Jumper cables clank to the ground

"I've finally done it now!"

He says smiling and putting down the red paintbrush while his luchadorian monster struggles on a reflective table vainly

This is the last moment where I can just sit here helplessly crosslegged

Meditation in search of some hidden cosmic vibration

While the paperwork for my bent smiles' parking permit is filled out by someone else

Even rolling around in my own filth has lost its taboo luster by now

The ink stains all the hands but my own cleaned fingers

My lack of experiential filth and my lack of real meat reality to chew on

I scratch them onto wooden tables at bars where people full of true destruction try to drown

Afraid that anyone of them might single me out for lacking the real fury

At night I hear the humpback whales blowing their ram horns

But I wake up in the dirt still sleeping in a pile with the coyotes

These things are what I talk about manically nonstop shackled to my gnawed funnybone

The words sprout from my mouth like weeds in the cracks on a green stone tennis court

The questions jut out of my arms like cactus spine syringes

With only half of the sharp thing visible it's just a quest

"Question:

If money and sex are the powers keeping most men
strong

Then why do I feel like I could chop down a
mountain with my words alone

when I have had so little of either lately?

Answer:

Because those are the big drugs

The granddaddy opiates

And if one has not opened the door for them more
than a little crack then

They could not possibly be rampaging in the
bloodstream now could they?"

He adjust his bowtie and sits back down behind his
briefcase

"No further questions your honor, the suspect
clearly has delusions of mediocrity"

So in my ignorance of all important truths I am of an
iron mind

Steel apologizing for no reason to the chicken neck being lopped off

I'm sorry if my tetanus bootspurs ever cut you

I never wanted anyone to bleed their secrets onto my tastebuds

I hold onto this masochistic eucharistic sadness

If only to keep the awful silence out of my eyelashes

Off of my drugless but somehow junkielike hollow chest

I tap graffiti strewn bathroom stall walls with my chewed to the cuticle fingertips

Listening to the pages in a book flipping like dove wings but making no cooing noises

"I always felt sorry for the pigeons when I gave them bread

And they didn't even know the difference between wonderbread and good jewish rye

But I gotta keep the moments from the in between from getting to me like fresh squeezed antifreeze"

He closes his trenchcoat and strides off taking big busy steps leaving shitty bootmarks on the jury's faces

I could have gone for it today, you know

I saw the headlights and the fog, the light in the refrigerator

I saw a fire extinguisher in a locked cabinet

Saw the way the sidewalk curved away off into some fake oblivion

Saw the way the nettles try to creep up between the slabs

I could have done it today

I could have gone for it

When I met that street performer with the guitar

And sang with him in front of a condemned deli

About hollis brown who lived on the outskirts of town

While he (Aaron his name was Aaron) played 2 low chords over and over on the strings

I could have followed that path until it went off into the sand

And slept on the rocks and the cacti

Lived momentarily in the wind like a dried leaf skittering insectile dysfunction

"Infected the whole time", the morticians speak softly and hold black derby hats to their shaved chests

Solemnly I swear I didn't build the atomic typewriter

It just landed groaning and hot on my front lawn one day and I didn't even listen to it when it told me to touch it

I didn't listen even when the doctors plotted against me outside the door while my mother nodded in approval

I didn't listen when they screamed STOP like it was a cork to be thrown down my gullet

And all the ketchup bottles were shattered on the bathroom floor

I could have gone for it, you know

I could have gotten moving today

Packed up my can openers and letter openers and bottle openers and left the refrigerator lonely

I could have sped off into the dusk as if it was waiting for me

Died in the silence and woken up somewhere noisier than here

But no

 The tourists fuck eachother sensible on beds of nails and the shreds of the last groups who were here last night

Changed by maids nightly used to lowering themselves on winches and wenches over the shark tank

"The clouds are quiet today, I wish you would say something

Have you noticed the way the clouds don't worry about touching each other?

When I float off I want to stay floating and never rain back down on my old parade"

He says, she says in a ping pong game between paraplegics in glued to the floor wheelchairs

 "Not today, not tonight, not ever Copernicus, I'm tired and have a headache so go discover the heavens yourself"

She rolls over and goes to sleep and the dog creeps up to her very late

And staringly he imagines eating her face instead of being a good boy

Not tonight not tonight not tonight the record skips waiting for bobby jean to surrender

Tonight the paper or plastic monster stays asleep, still chained to his addictions

Tonight is for eating rotten apples and wiping the sweat from my piggy forehead like condensation on a beer glass

But when summer comes

      (Take a deep breath and try to feel the first sparks of spring on your cheeks)

I'll follow that path into wordlessness and a green lie

The Best Kind Of Machine, a confession

Now I'm not catholic

In fact the nuns cross themselves when I wink at them

But the concept of confession, of feeling decent
only because you tore off the scabs

Well, it just makes my scabby jewboy hips quiver

Insurance policies for the dead have the possibility
to gather unlimited interest

Buy up as many as you can, prices get radioactive
rather quickly

Let the ritual begin, hoist those porkchops

Chefs and surgeons test the broth cautiously with
their pinky toes

A barn radio coughs out the dust of boiled giraffes
while the little children laugh

The market is up today but let's all try to control our
hyenic anticipations, hmm?

Now gentlemen of the jury, don't leave the
operating theater before you see how much blood
I've poured into this production

How many quivering muscle black-mass YMCA
dance crazes I've flippantly butchered

A mound of chicken bones demonstrates the difference between Colonel Sanders and Genghis Khan

My advice to you posthistoric petticoat tyrants

When the colonoscopy train comes whistling through the wall have your grimaces rehearsed

There might be humor now but in thirty years I doubt the longevity of it

Hitchhikers perch on the boundaries smoking patriotism wrapped in crow feathers

Man that empire better be a metaphor or we are eff you see kay ee dee taxidermy

I wish I could ladle out a blue sound with my fingers, the prison sentence trails off

The best kind of machine,

Intones the starved out jazzdreamed patient zero, broken fingers all in plaster casts

Wouldn't know he was a machine, got me?

I can't snap, but

Sometimes I get suspicious, the mood goes green

It peeks through crystalline keyholes at other superstitious twitches

When the time comes and the seaturtles are in heat

I can get you a discount on the antiseptic highdive yolks

He'd just, go about his business and leave it steaming on the grass

I intuit futures as a concrete mad travelling salesman in a music-man hat

Walking lamphue illuminated suburbs ruminating on the number of footsteps left

And passing on sad-sack orally fixated traditions of genetic detritus

So there I was, riding my mule on the shoreline

When outta the seashell hums this gal in a polkatoothed bikini

And she says to me, "There's a fella back there who wants my secret recipe so you'd better get rescuing me"

So I said, "sweetheart this is the 25th century and I am in a monogamous satanic pact with this mule so, rescue yourself"

But I see why you wanted that recipe, made her into one hellofa soufflé

Now hold this cable here for just a sec while I adjust the tape measure

Ick change the channel this old dude makes me soft and chokey

Atomic bigbands honk wheatfields in the crater of someday

That was the sound of buzzbombed optimism and shaved metallic honeycombs

Standing spinal to the gleam promised smokestack

Calm before pushing arms into frenzied semantic sharkchurns

There's going to be a moment you've felt before

A static hush we lie there on stained sheets after
sex discussing a mutual lust for fame

When you make a choice, these yellow spectacles
are affecting my hearing

The noise should be pure, cerulean

I picture one of my possibilities

Saccharine rags wringing gasoline by the drop

In the tunnel lips of New York City

Briefcase full of smirking miracles

Pointing westward towards the saxophone
graveyard

They always toss their holy tricksters into volcanic
has been holes in the ozone

I hope to choose the side of titans, instead of your
sterile hymns

I'd have the curved lip of Elvis instead of Saint Paul's
pompadour

Spewing gourmet ambulances round charcoal
corners

All I remember is the ice, pain is temporary and
ethereal

Teeth loosened in electric sockets upon impact

It's only a solar needle, don't look, I know it's bright

It might sting a little, like turning a record over to
side two

When I opened that door miles below astorian
tombstones

I set out to find real deserts and oceans and all I got
were puddles and sunburns

Screaming for naked heatstroke before the
chainlink gates of city hall

Ignoring the momentary borealis roar always heard
just before spoonfuls of winter sleep prescriptions

Just a slight little bee buzzing in your ear, that's all

Choice or not, hunger remains the primary concern

You'll know perfectly well when to reach for it

So this then is my confession, served hot, vague and
hemorrhaging

I comprehend like a foreign opera engraved onto
the side of skyscrapers

Languages whose shells I can't crack from the inside
or otherwise

Beads of water slip up speeding glass

Accidentally dynamiting the therapy exit

Tractor tire sculpted soil edges a landfill heaped
with reaching mannequins

Cars fall like raindrops across the interstate

Valhalla Sodapop Ignition

The possible, el niño waited

Clad in folds of greener morning

Cornstalks shuffled in their plaguemunched nervous way

Genderless mute scarecrow on the hilltop

I huff shove puffed upwards

But when I got there, empty sandals

Dusksplit stones stared in raindrop lost details

Half a platoon of mangled soldiers drooling pomegranate, they don't look so bad to me

Spread the leaves on their chests and set them afloat

Trace them in windex and follow them well

I'm leaving these instructions indecipherable on the urinal wall

Please, send the remains of my silk shirt to Freya

She understands the way of the weaved breeze

And won't shirk the responsibility of burning

A comet appeared, flashing modestly glinting paradoxes

My only remaining duty is to follow an easter-island voice towards western shouts

In this version of the fable (and there are many)

I lobbed a blue egg into a shimmering swimming pool

Molotov blackmail kerplunk

And when the nurses plucked the microchip from under my skin

I almost heard it hmm hmmm humming

Thumbing a ride to escape the rising liquid consequence

Calling a secret name into well rounded blacktrain subway tunnels the echo ichor ripple

These arid honeysuckle depths hint at less sickly nectars

So the sand miners union engraved cautiously

Just past the crabgrass and bronze plaques on the gates of city hall

Here lies the big one, don't tapdance too hard or he
might wake up

Leukimial wheels in motion suggest a moth yawn
nightgowned stumbler to dig dig dig

If only the idea were true that there are seven suns
above of which we only see the one

An imperial desert waits to the west spreading dune
fungus

Slow cactus paralysis beneath the coat of an
authentic egyptian tarantella salesman

I never understood the spiral arm gesture

The whole drama would have been solved if
Sherlock had put a bullet in Moriartys' kneecap first
thing

Still, amorphous future song stalactites drip from
the celing, one for you and one for me

Limping, the parched owl lost his spectacles

Where's your awards ceremony now?!

I botched the moment, butchered the test run

Tattled on the gasoline grope

So soon, they will lay us down soft and spoonfeed a creationary memoir

Milk-cured intravenous

Though today all you know are spires of soot and wonder

First there was sound (and I've said this before)

Then there was a sea (open wide)

Then a sky (or a promise of one)

Then a seed (way beneath where it feels too nice to look and spoil everything)

Then a mountain (slowdanced with toothaches)

Then a forest, so tremble

A smokestack hiccup jet fever winks knowingly

At the start of the game, all the adoring spectators carried signs that said vote for Jesus not christ

You know it sipping warm beer from a green bottle

Know it like a hunger pang

It's time to return (so they say)

To that gravity shunning vomitwide tendril of blue

Lungs full of hush

Playing cards shredded royally flushed hand in the cookie jar

I never take these deadlines seriously

The thimble of clear liquor

Because there are barriers beyond yellow tape put up to keep squatters out, walls I can't pass

Tonight was supposed to be for clicking lighter flames to leafpiles

Maybe when I'm young again I'll understand

Why the German prime minister telling her pet immigrants to shape up or ship out

Made me want to croon it had to be yoooouuu in a grin of Dracula catharsis

What travesty is this that the kids don't revere the beard of Colonel Sanders anymore?

This was, like much else, predicted in retro viewmaster musings

I'm writing this letter to tell you, yay heavily

Sugarfiend got the electric armchair

So when you make the arcade pilgrimage

Step carefully over his snaking cardiogram jump-ropes

Melting caramel on the basement carpet

Little sparrows open their pierced beaks wide and expectant

Yellow food packages fall from theoretic helicopters after the mushroom storm cloud sands

But there are just too many hamburger angels sprawled sleepy on the fire-escape stairwell

And I've never had enough to solve this iron maiden ruby rubix cube

And trying to chew out the virus just itches

Perhaps I'll go bonkers for the nearest lightswitch

A sudden leap of machinery in faith

Reach for the remote and just hope it has batteries

These acid popped voyeuristic tendencies always
get the best of me

These words are razors to my wounded heart

What a fucking drama queen I just can't believe he
said that

And I can't take off my pants in public, though I
want to sometimes

But you don't hear ME complaining about it and
showing everyone my stumps

The closest was when I took off my shoes and
walked the last mile home barefoot

Sized up very suspiciously by suburban housewive
minivan amputees

There's just so much to lear and forget inside this
skull full of mead

Time to get to work at the bumpersticker factory

Listen, I think this FatElvis microphone is on

So if any of you wannabe Van Goghs can't hear just chuck an ear at me

In the year of your lord 1054 a great light shined from above

Chinese astronomers kept meticulous records

We know now that it was a supernova

Not a divine nervous breakdown

Just stars dying quiet as churchmouse winos ruptured in the cold

I don't ever want to reach that trashbag flopped shoreline, even the path smells like meat

White lines count the whooshing centipede miles

I was nearly run over by a supergiant semi truck carting cows

Sixty mile per hour caged bovine

Fossil fueled short term pleasure

Behind door number one your number two fantasy is growling and growing impatient

Where we're going scythes and legs are needed

A very long time ago we threw water balloons across the street at eachother

Remember how they neon splatted our delight on the concrete?

Kiss me spinning with a mouthful of drillbits, what's your name again?

The only way I hold onto mine is with the letters from insurance companies

Assuring that I JUST missed the magic hour

Silly rabbit, trying to steal credit for the great hypnotism

Waiting for a surprise in the mail every day for a month

We slept dreamless near the tombstone, giddy for further instructions

Not sure what, that's what makes it a surprise

No good can come of this earthen ticking snow flaked in someday thinned hair

Turn on the device it's time for another latex learning experience

Quick quick the lullaby is wearing off!

On television I saw footage of a woman being kicked in the head at a teaparty rally

The man who did it says the camera angle made it look worse than it was

When politics prevail the boots of angry fat walmart managers sound like a riverdance

His amigos stood in a circle as he put his best foot forward

And she looked on in typical liberal shithead disbelief

And my woefully effective memory preserves every ohfuckno wasptwitch horror

Election day is never as nasty as it seems and I hope that stays true

Mystic hooey will never be a legitimate political party

In this toetapping ritual crop rotation

I hold onto the root of thunder radiating rust coronal glare

Spark moonbeam cream soda aspiration inhalation

The weight shifts and even the elephants swoon in this fading summer

Bed springs creak self-consciously alone

I binoculate hurricane painkillers

As my never ever sweetheart sweets naked on the telephone

There are new doors with broken peepholes everywhere

But are any home like this one?

Crow circle (there he goes again) the bonfire Arizonan squawk message from your mother radio

Something approached down the pipeline

I just wanted a stomp power outage airconditioned telegram choked with YES

To sail on, change jangle, bulb filament silver waves

To planecrashing comprehension

Strung revved up bubo cornflakefield gumlines

Lamp post steel cools the snipersweat beaded
forehead

I told you I don't have what it takes

Whatever alien charisma is necessary to survive at
this altitude

Though perhaps I have the wormbait oomph
remaining

To crack the glass stasis saltwater safe combination

Turn the wheel and aim the crossbow engine
trajectory

Something new, numbers glow hot on the doorknob

I turn the key

A pair of willfully ambiguous emerald hardened
binomial eyes

Swim thunk through smudged stainedglass
lighthouse panes

Something new

I turn the key

3 questions

Did Alice look upon the engine

      knowing she had braved it's rolling gears
and snaky orange coils before?

Or did she

      naively thrust her arm forward into the oily
unknown?

And if she knew that she had faced down the
spinning pointless mechanisms so many times

      did she push on anyway?

We smoke nothingness out of empty buckets with curtains shut and walls covered in crayon marks

The possibilities rush bloody to my head as I search for the timed blinking of her eye

Knitting and knitting, macaroni funeral shrouds

Clumping into the restroom at a McDonalds

Are we ready?

He

Doesn't ask questions, only takes out canisters full of them

Slams

So much nosebleed brightness for a moment demanding quiet pillboxes

Down

Horseraced, terminally snickering   trite hunger

The jackhammer of equanimity

Nightvision switch kicking in filament
transformatory

Eleven at night, closing time in an hour and my
shoes sound loud on the scrubbed floors

Not sure why I'm here, a momentary wave of
nausea or nostalgia perhaps

A snort of propane and perfume, we only sell
cardboard crowns here

I came to this city in the sand expecting black-
leather Kool-Aid

Across boardwalks where I could hear the sea but
not see it and carnivorous cityhalls

To find the visionary gene pool of failed architects

Stacked as high up as they go low, cats dart in
between toxic lightsockets

Trashcans floating through space, yeah this is
progress

Somehow, we haven't perfected the technology

Velocity approaching maximum absurdity

And most toilets have that quarter inch of decay between them and the linoleum

Between the apparatus and the antiseptic tall tale:

Four mercury-pricked angels entered my body through carcrash tinted tearducts

I have unraveled the swagger and now sweat consequences

Say something serious now, we don't have all week to wait for your alleged virus to sprout

Pogostick into the forgotten ice-cream flavor

Headache simmered drift epileptic disco medicine ball

A luxury cruiseship full of frightened walrus minded millionaires over a roar of niagra engine celebrations

I recognize the Rosicrucian narcotics agent by the tattooed plans on his pale shoulder

The deepfried dagger trembles musically

Bong-hits of Haitian earthquake

Televised juicy live pandemic of tainted sweatpants

Unbuttoned poppoppop anticipates a
microwaveable suspension of gravity

The adolescent pharaoh's gold clown feet kicked,
once

And the rope groaned soul exit stage left on a
faberge neck

Federal schoolgirls vulture under his twitch with
wickerbaskets full of bats

Broad shoulders breathe like black bagged lungs

Perception split atom twins

Oh but the nails sure are SWEET

Each eye lazing in a different oasis

Marathonic huffing gardens of voodoo tomatoes

Audible altitude of a gushing bite, I bring you this
gift of fragrant concussion

The fields with stretch on gusty with chunks of
concrete ghost sirens poking out of hilltops

A shepherd only learns his real purpose when the sheep run out of grass

A car horn blares, feelin ok in there buddy?

Two red headed seven year old boys lick popsicles in their endless June swelter

While farther down their trainwhistle timelines

Split lip iron blooms of industry faked floral orgasms

Dud firecrackers fuse to bacterial nova vacuum cleaners

Finally the lush of former springs slips a green hand down my cheekbones

Patient gasps on a cold silver screen table, we're losing the spark

The purpose of this pyramid experimental scheme

I find no forests, only a heat wave stopsign redder at dusk

The goal (don't laugh, I know your works) is to clone time, it's the only currency worth anything

Recreate the moment and hope it doesn't fang the rose-stem

I vaguely recall a net dipping into sedated waters,
moonlight drips everywhere

God and man evolve in the same way

With same flaw of lethal intelligence we both give in
at the end of the cycle

Possibly circular, Quetzalcoatl flees into the sky

Or possibly, intelligence is a fatal dead end genetic
pile-up

We make our successors gaze upwards with
blemished circuits

We evolve until we disappear, leaving behind a trail
of spat black mythic pomegranate seeds

A recipe for cooking the ecstasy of reptiles

Raspberry dribble the liquid of my name
from your tongue

I want it to stick out like the magnificent chunks of
what five minutes ago was a smooth snowglobe

Nectar five hundred yard dash venom

Split lightbulb shines temporarily

Coil inside hissing singing meat-hook

My savage inability to comprehend

Is neither noble nor ghastly

I wear a crown of nettles to remind me

Of the omnipresent choice

Between the primal thump and the electric hum

First there was sound

Flip the switch off

And there is THAT MOMENT struggling

Trapped insectile zapping a projectile idea: I was made of fireflies then

Gift-wrapped in extension cords

Recklessness only gets us to the wall earlier, then what?

      The canaries wear gas masks round here

Digging for birdseed synonymous with ascension

      But if I could unplug my body odor

I would I would

Take a dull ax and split the Hiroshima willow

Fill a notebook with shards

      I can read to you a bedtime story

Goodnight moon, goodnight sky, goodnight flies

Goodnight all you lonely astronauts

You sweaty illuminations are spit-shined

I cannot say what needs to be said when all is said and done

I spout a gold plate collector's edition cliché

And give you the gentlest boot I have to kick with

So with the oven preheated and hungry

I bake something sweet, perhaps a big cake

Make sure you put the stripper in AFTER you've cooked it

First: carve a perfect angel from fossils

Then jackhammer it back to particles

And loudly vacuum the dust with your juiciest machine

Pour out the teargas-canisterish bag

And stomp until your toes are ashy

Lie down and make a crematorium snow-angel

FINALLY snort that until your nose bleeds

Ignore the shaky hand gripping your touristic sensibilities

We can show them, show them all

How to stitch puncture wounds with scotch tape

Turn to page seven for metric conversions and
baptisms

Measure the rope juuuuuust right

Pick a flea from your arm hair

See it leaping blue between the prong and the wall

I would give them all my pollen

Give them, give thee

Give freely

The iron stutter stumbles

A wonder! That's it!

Give me migraine thunderous applause

Give me a new name

One that tastes like a champion's last touchdown

Read that name to me swiftly

But leave a few teeth intact please

Deep yawn here comes the boot

You are to me

As strong as the dedicatory moment after a sunset

When I can see the whole sky sunless indigo and
unruined by fear of blinding

Briefly it's all mine

It's mine before we speak our sculpted goodbyes

(All this and more can be yours if you call the
number at the bottom of your screen in the next

Ten minutes for just seven ninety nine, that's right
seven ninety nine but hurry supplies are limited!)

Then

Nothing

Except the scraping of blankfaced statues

Sucked or shoved down open manholes

Yellow caution tape be damned

     The holes in the whole façade

Punch satellite pinholes through canvas

I had the entire quartz cloud in my arms

Water those bleary eyes and perhaps a tree will
sprout ripping them open

Are they my eyes or yours?

      Regardless of eventual answers

We will never drift leafy onto fields of nostalgia

To lie there waving and sneezing

That door remains closed to me now

I can only kneel on this clean carpet

Peeking through the keyhole

And a shaded vexing oasis

Mumble my farewells and send them out like desert
island bottle messages

Goodnight all you lonely astronauts

All you wounded cowboys

All you sober writers and melted firefighters

Goodbye all you quick witted hypnotists

Goodnight all you boys we wanted to become

A cowardly vein shivers in my temple

The lightbulbs don't dare shine here

Even though I claim

To see the difference

Between knowing and seeing

Between seeing and feeling

Between feeling and knowing

First there was sound

Light the candelabra with strike-anywhere matches

And toss their smoking bones to the marble floor

Hidden sounds

There are sentences and articulations on the very
edge of breath

Hydraulic calculatory umbilical sensations

Stutterings that remain unspoken, pressed tightly
into an iceberg clump of noise

Sometimes when I haven't said anything in hours I
worry that in silence I have forgotten how to speak

Dark grass against a blank tangled pink of summer
sky

Sagebrush air minueting on your hardened eyelash

I climbed a grey mountain that grew more massive
with every footstep

And drank the unmelted snow that waits clean
under the cool of graffiti red stones

Though I grasp to the branches for your song, you
are not my nightingale

The choice of where to jump is scalpel-strung
between rivers

Gushing unshaped southward, the gust of primitive
rests cold upon my lips

Deconstructing Dame Vera

When I listen to Vera Lynn

Promising that we'll meet again

I picture her (in black and white film)

Undernourished and blond

Dressed in a cloth paler than her nineteen-thirty-nine pallor

Flapping her hand goodbye in a sootspat subway
station miles underneath the blitzkrieg

Machines rumbling their coal stomachs above and
below

Sunny days and bluebirds through seven decades of
soil and steam

Smiling through promises that remain fictional, I'm
still waiting

For that dull zapcat sprawling electric current

Teardrop sunbeamed noise

To careen through the tunnels

Burning smooth among the sanguinary fascist lilies

4 clanks (an origami poem)

1

               You have such a citric chuckle

Smoke fingers twirl

Machinery of sky

Intimidates silver and exquisite doubt

Clank! Clouds blank memory spark

Wheels turn glass eyelashes

                 Tear pages from a gilded book

2

Smoke machinery intimidates clank! Wheels

Fingers of silver clouds turn

You twirl sky and blank glass

Have exquisite doubt, memory-spark eyelashes tear

Such a citric chuckle, pages from a gilded book

3

Smoke fingers, you have such

Machinery of twirl, exquisite citric

Intimidates silver sky, doubt chuckle

Wheels clank! turn blank spark

Glass eyelashes tear from a gilded book

4

Clank! Smoke machinery intimidates glass wheels

Fingers of silver clouds turn eyelashes

You twirl skies and pages

Doubting the spark of gilded memory

Tear an exquisite chuckle from a blank book

Contemplating the crossroads

I'm standing at the crossroads baby & I believe I'm sinkin down- Robert Johnson

When you contemplate it strongly

All roads

Are crossroads

They hold within them

Sighing angular possibilities

But most roads

Like us

Have lost the purity of gravity and dust

The hiss of ice pellets melting in the weeds after a hail storm

A plywood cross wreathed in wilted marigolds, stuck in the mud

A photograph of a boy with a crewcut taped to it

Smiling and left there

Not here, not here

The foot tapping intersections of gasoline perfumed metropolises

Have thieved so many with steel and promise

That nobody remembers the wreck of their laughs

Nullifying the civilized sacrifice

Somewhere there are seagulls

And a scoop of icecream falls plop from a cone

We did not construct them

We merely uncovered them

Pulled aside a clean white sheet

Gave them a chunk of our hunger

A thimble of fever

Eventually we go down

Hoping deeply to sleepwalk back home

Lugging a new guitar case

I turn sunburned with the west behind me

No houses or barking dogs

And all the headlights are drifting away

Gripping a dirtclod

Tight with déjà vu

Let it drop

Piece by cloudy piece, hush

An evening of orange peels descends

A licorice-winged raven on a freshly painted
fencepost

Streetlamps try to push it back, flutter

I contemplate the crossroads

Devoid of flashlight comfort

Desiring to catch the flash of a thunderbolt, sudden
on my reflective teeth

Quickly now

I am caught **quickly** now, as if a speck of dust riding
unsure on a rubberband midsnap

Were to **stop** itself **and wonder** why prior to being
overtaken by **the squeal**

In the eyeballed force of momentum, there is an inert
lack **of suspicion**?

What if upon waking you discovered every door in that
big ugly house to be unlocked and thrown wide open?

I've been following following following my own
magnifying glass anthill inferno footsteps

The first bite into a ripened mango is **deeper and
brighter** than the next

Stop and feel the spin, oblivious **beneath** your hand

Would you take the time to look through **each keyhole**
or would you just go straight into the brass unknown?

                            Hopping **full throttle** click of
a dry throat through waterbottle forests

Over felled logs and cairns built to try and please jealous
dope-**peddling gods**

Yours may be vengeful but mine is **green** and cares not
for **railroad spikes**

The old fury
bearded oaks form archways into chlorophyllic **realms of nectar**

Still I **burn giddy** and those behind me
bellow and those **ahead of me** laugh crash

Drifting tangle through the screamless clouding
smokestack ocean amplification of **space**

We should become as one **jetfire apparatus** gleaming
with **the sound** of unplucked thighs **and** harps

Threading vomitorious **chunks of nebulae**
through hypodermic **spools**

But your roaring hands, they were here with me through
most of these floods **working the loom**

Floating impossible **twitch** the
generator smells of **ozone** and carbohydrates

Twitch **the sickness**

Twitch the cure

Twitch the **fishhook** and the sparkling lure

The liar's broken strings no longer hum along **catatonic**
to platonic tectonic erotic impossibilities

Lift the paradox on the backs of befouled stain glass
devotees and feel it shudder as we approaches a center

You followed a **dove** up there wanting to find **the blue**

You found a **blown out** tire

And ignored the slick smacking flame-hungry oil patch of taunting **progress**

                                        Suddenly they all
AHAAA! into one another

The grass beneath **my unwashed hair reaches upwards** as high as its hands allow

There is a limit to every reach but I intend to stretch my **quicksilver** arm starward

And brush away the grubs carrying my vision who curl around **nightlights** secretly

They burrow noctophobic into every daydream, every lick of icecream, every matchstick **flicker**

                        This one is red and mean and this one's lips **quiver** with soured kindness

In this one I dive with patient **seaturtles down** among the gagged choir

Shipwrecks **fill the holes** in my teeth

Beneath the lobotomized **separation** of desire from scorchmarks

A reason tingles in **the scoliosis** of my evolved spinal organum

I give **you** this **riddle** to play with:

To know me you must **learn** and **to** learn me you must already know me, **what am I?**

Drink me like eager wine when the clock turns three

When we were smiling reptiles, **we remembered** and made a choice to forget

And now want **the popped bubble** back shining translucent lucid

When the timer ticks to twelve, we **will taste** nothing but vinegar again

I turn mad and **piggy** on the pollinated wheels of my own sneezed wants

The changing from this to that is **almost** tangible

Here, we are silent and our heads don't turn

Here, **the owls watch** with one sleepy cataract from the rafters

These cathedrals tolerate **nothing** less than robed servitude to their termites

But **there,** through one of those fresh picked portcullises
there is **possibility**

       Possibly the holy **crack** of the baseball-**bat**
destructive down a windowless hallway

That **little boat** is capsizing and bucketing out the sludge
only slows down the slide towards being another acrylic

Hanged in the museum, feet still **twitching** for the
tourists to ooo and ahhh and take pictures with

But there is always **the possibility of** opening one's way
straight into a field without farmers or steel

       Where **a dandelion** glow
growing **novas between** my crunchy **lightning** fingers

Symbiosis

I read a news article on my computer

Saying that the last tiger could be gone by 2012

A small blurb on yahoo, safe from any roaring flesh

A scoured prophetic electronic landscape

I didn't have to really do more than skim it though

Some things you just know lifetimes ahead

White snow screened rose up all drained of
pouncing

Sterilized except for the cookie crumbs and
beerbottles scattered on my bedroom floor

And all these books full of overexplored old friends
lounging moldy

When the final fanged intruder stomps his last prey,
razoring ballerina ferocity

Hunger incomparable to our own red streak

Will there be enough tragedy in comfort to slow the
wheels to a quick and painless growl?

In my circular daydreams the doctors nod
sympathetically

Sharpening pitchforks for the villagers in the
backroom hospital poolhall

And hours after the feast, worshippers wait in the
black-Friday cold

Shivering anticipatory outside lightless stores

Mystified as oldworld raggy pilgrims gazing up at
godhouse pyramids

A sudden vertigo stumble will neckpop the
fearlessly sallow future

I never intended to end up looking at kitchen knife
displays more than as an occasional treat

The joke's on the blunted errand boy

No cell phone reception in a redwood consignment
casket

And nobody knows morse code anymore

Aww how cute, those jiggling secondclass
backbones

Don't know funny until it's sticking between their ribs

Obviously, a streaming coinfilled rustwell is the only non-nauseating pixel

And the art museums are stuffed with taxidermied rebel causes

Go on touch em, their dictatorial genitals are just fossilized snickers

I am spoonfed an elephantine truth by one hand

And forcefed a sweetypie fib from the other

Quietly, I reached for the clock but it was too high up to get at

Ticking extinction for the second best predator on earth is now a foregone conclusion

George Washington's coal bits wet-dream breakfast cereal

As sure as the Berlin shadowpuppets follow a click click boom flashlight command

There were no lions in Iraq and believe you me we tried

Pardon my politically flatulent posturing

But Pax-Americana only lasted fifteen years

Fleetingly we were the uncontested top dynamite shit-heap sheepdog

The numbers never coagulated

And in one generation (T minus Y ignition)

When the kids looks out onto their smaller sliver of unknown joy

They will see only matchsticks and desire to become torchbearers

Not that I've ever seen a tiger in the wild, or been in a real wyrd jungle

Only at zoos or designated hiking trails still focusing on what preservation will consume me

Pacing nervous in my well furnished cage, it's getting worse now

The paradise machine parachute factory is just about out of fuel

Puffing orange and black fumes

Wear a ski-mask when you leave, the sugar-smog is feeling bold

Eating the old ways (all of them) would be oh so rude and presumptuous

All the wincing green is shrunken, even vegetarians need to eat

That which covered continents in a permanent aetheric sneeze, plugged

Great white way shark attacks on the Florida coast have hit an all time high

They tell me these things easily, the pills are smooth and round like stones

A garbage isle swirls industrially gleaming ejaculatory bile

Bulldozed their Sherwoods and set eventually butchered cows loose among the stumps

Skinned off their pelts so as to know what design to replicate for fireplace rugs

Here's a bandaid now get back to work those files won't alphabetize themselves

Belching nowhere near extinguished inflated
coronary herds

No more Tonys or Tiggers or whatever cuddly
corporate deity it is you pray to

The obituary of the "great god Pan" was premature
by millennia but correct nonetheless

With innocence mistaken for rapist-smiling

And vultures prolifically crouched in the Vatican
outhouse

I wanna climb the ironlunged hills

And wheeze sickness down on cities birthed for cars
not feet

But my rage is only a drooly flicker of the
gangrenously beautiful

Bite sized morsel mortgage engagement ring
bonfire

I wouldn't know a real clean heat until it scorched
my sarcastic eyebrows

So let's play a nice game of spin the barrel to pass
the time

Whoever lights the fuse and strikes the homerun
blackeyed sulfurhead, gets a secret name

A slick dolphinous coup de tattoo

The tin fisted orangutan repoman always flails first

I want this juvenile prehensile age of precocious
steamrollers paving the way for nursing homes

To put down the heybaby bottle of superstitiously
expensive pixiedust

Having risen up (Look who thinks his walkman in the
reincarnation of Syd Barret haw haw haw)

Now cometh the customary slide back into
lobotomized indentured and insured servitude

It was closer this time, the listening breath on the
other side of the wallpaper

It's not my choice to knock five times, rarely ever is

Closer, but not enough to withdraw proper
amounts of X-rayed inhibition

We're storing the stuff for winter so if you hear
squealing it's just the new glass ceiling settling

This is the sound of a former hunter stepping off
into gunless suburban fogbanks

Maybe next time the tigers won't get caught in the
toothless armchair crosshairs

The plug got yanked without painkillers, only one
volt milked

In my self induced ipecac visions that come mewling
like waves of spraypaint

I walk, a humble student of emerald loves through
unafraid forests

With the poison escaping out my veins instead of
into them

The surgical separation anxiety all but symbolically
complete

I can't apologize because some languages run
deeper than syllables

Maybe next time

Symbiotically there will be one pure eight limbed
willow

And the choice will be mine, not made for me

Perhaps next time

Not Quite

I only remember it vaguely   breathing on my neck

When I feel a luminescence   on my
shoulders, warm and heavy

I almost remember   like a taste of honey fading
from chapped lips

When I hold dust in my hands and let it drop out   in a
cloud

The noise is on the tip of my ears sucking in air and
preparing to whisper

The cacophony of engines with nearly rusted legs spread
drowns   the exhale of a blossom dropping from a branch

Two pale blue dreams   shivering
holding up the sky

Fail to create but   cannot undo their mistake

A dragonfly
over a lake of algae

Two marble pillars grow from my eyesockets

                                    They are from me yet I don't
own them

                    They belong to the temple's burned out
body

For it is clouds who keep the
mountain floating

Spun into fine strands of dustbitten merry-go-rounds

On one side of this   forest

The sun has turned viewable red   and is
blushing

That object of so much   abstract worship

Hemorrhaging   the last   of the warmth   from
wavelength fingertips and dropping gently from green
cheeks

The last drops   of the ultraviolet wine   are
being spilled down   quivering chins   into the soil

Peering through   foliage with binocular moonshine
eyelids

A fairy tale   is tattooing   itself into   existence
with one fully formed branchy hand   holding the needle

The drunken proto-angel
tripped and   stabbed the sand

A family of oaks   grew from the spot   and his
tears watered them to terrible heights

Threatened by the suicidal shining of a toy sword

A chalk outline

Out on the farthest hills from   these green
shores

A leaf sailed to the edge of the branch and was forgotten

On the other
side   of the forest

Even the grandfather stones with their wide eyed myth-
bones grow rust and moss   in the cold years

Yesterday's prizewinning
moon   is   awakening, frosty and perfect

A woman in a silver   ocean gown

Pushes my ribbon-pinning hand away
smiling icily   almost
nicely

The
stars play   supernova   piano melodies for her

A holey
boardgame   with a few rules   and cardboard pieces

And in the middle of a   natural unsteamrolled clearing
in the   multifaced   forest at the edge

In-between   the   infinite
moment   and the   coming hunger   of a windy dusk

We have stopped   stomping on 5
leaf   clover   dancefloors

All around us   are   trees   with
fruit   too high to reach

So we lie back on the grass and wait for   the drums
marching from somewhere proud and cloudy

We drink   the smile
from a tangerine sunset and listen

A definition

Once more I wake to the sound of ringing bells

A shining slick ice-cream traffic cone impossibility

3 faces in the morning, dressed for a funeral

Starlight gives no myth for free

Paris gives the shellacked apple to not-so-green
Venus

And within a week planes painted with swastikas

Were dropping crates full of booby-trapped telescopes

Over Babylon's department stores

Crowded with know-it-all astrophysicists

Space needle hypodermic head rushes

Trampled on the banks of an investment polluted river

A cloud, out loud, a shroud, underground

Put my wish between your birthday candles

In your lungs and on your field of alpha-wave negative vegetables

Water them with knee-scrape bandaids

I see it, hanging from a thorny branch

Napalm lip gloss fruit of my refused labor

I can never push far enough, you know that

Circling satellite around a blue mother

Back to the moon, permanently ethereal

Oxidized gambler bets there's nothing funny

About rolling blackout aphrodisiac amok swamp
slurpers

When the whizz kid pisses out his special grimace

Nobody expects us to sniff the concrete

Wanting to be pirates yo ho ho

No more crossed wires in my tin whistle coffin
kindling

What I'm TRYING to say

Through all this jazzacular migration

Is that I was asked to define love

By an existentially challenged English major

In denial of their words' heat

So I'll say this through a huff of second hand
chimney smoke

I've only experienced something close

A few scrawny times

Each of them sad and dripping gorgeous

Like morning glories covering a rusted guillotine

I'll never be some alpha male gamma hulk

Arrow in the heel conquering hero demanding a heil

Nor do I want to be

Some spark tongued moron with an authentic
demonic swagger

Pull the belt tight around your waist

Perhaps try to reconstitute

A snowflake of memory, ever so repetitive

The scent of a passing garbage truck

The scrape of a foot on the sidewalk

Broken glass attempting aurora borealis

The plastic bag half in the sand

Half flapping in a sterile breeze

I traveled all this way, over all those fences

Wanting to give you back your forgotten boots

We coagulated temporary sunshine

I come close sometimes

But when I put my effervescent eye to the telescope

I get an old fashioned voodoo Neptune Pleistocene blinding

And every dawn someone I never see

Climbs a long stairway to the top of a bell tower

Yanks the rope to draw out the noise

And the dogs howl along

Calling the insomniac faithful, closer and closer

Circling the jazzman's airplane

Celestial lightbulbs sway on milky strings in a field of twilight

I hope that Glenn Miller's airplane is in orbit, circling the atmosphere

Though nobody remembers him now

They think rock & roll (which is really just a metaphor for America) will live forever

My my hey hey

Nothing's really here to stay

Not even the dangling hook, all shined temptation

Music hangs in air and ear for a minute or two

Then it's gone and there's only the recollection

Because despite pushing the repeat button or keeping photo albums

It's only the initial moment, the first time, which really matters

A story's pages smudge, yellow or are forgotten

And only the ashes of feeling stay

Crushed by the illusionary weight of time

I stare upwards

Not blinking until my eyes begin to water

I hope the pinholes of light I'm seeing

Are stars, not satellites

Cannibalized poem #8

A butterfly floated from an insectile cloud taller
than the mountain

Flapping wings like eyelashes

A nectar drinking yellow leaf the same color as your
hair disappeared downward

I wanted right then to give you a wind touched kiss

That's the feeling I want to remember into the depths of a long september

I can feel the roller coaster clicking it's way to the top of the tracks

Not in free fall yet but any minute this thing is gonna

Drop silent and violently

Like sweat in the bathtub

I can smell the carnival food rising off the asphalt

Horsecrap from the track on the breeze

Summer used to last forever when we were young

Everyone was endless, golden and green

Now I can hear the engines of my future starting up

Brushing their oily teeth and cracking metal knuckles

Getting ready for everything takes the place of doing anything eventually

No one sits on the swingset anymore and the seats creak emptily

Space filled with trinkets

Ah and in a thousand years of awkward progress

The 9 steps fulfilled

When humanity has killed its way to the stars we'll find that whoever lived on foreign worlds

Already annihilated themselves by a divine fire

Fiddle a sad song for tomorrow while plugging up laughter with a toilet plunger

Let us sit and watch the six legged sunset

No sickly grin crawls and no dismal future calls as long I'm holding your hand

And have I told you?

There is a hole in the back wall of my cave

Where the stars pour in like silver wine

That night I dreamed all my teeth fell out of their sockets and were planted in the soil

Roots detached from their desolate pink homeland

Great trees grew from them and touched the sky

And from the branches flew a butterfly

High noon in the temple of the sparrow

The cave dwellers in my skull

Are crayoning the walls, flags at half mast

And are stagnant, following the speedlimit

Staying in the lines

A dumpster with a dead dog's head

Hanging a german shepherd tongue over the side

Among the teacups, ashtrays and stale muffins

A wet kiss among the marigolds and chewed
chicken bones

Diving into a green swimming pool behind an
abandoned home

Rain gutter groaning gushy

Paint chip steel rooster turning

Climbing out in filthy blue jeans

A narcoleptic tattletale with open palms water stain

One of his eyes was so much bluer than the other

So much so much all the zap had gone out

As if it had stolen its partner's light

Hidden it deep below cracks in the rainless road

The sleeping sickness transmitted by dust devils
forbidden

Vision incision stitch, we all forget eventually

Flames on the riverside rivers on the fireside
extinguish surgery

Hieroglyph ember of remembrance

Or some semblance of citric bite

Squeeze peach juice, don't

Exhaust sticky sigh, forget

Metal chevy rusting in a pit, my friend

There are deserts beyond this one

Where I can grit my crooked teeth

Desiring to be lost mystical in the sand

Stagnant, amphibious and ambidextrous

Hexed, undersexed, deloused, overfed

Hyper-want incinerate confidence

Poking ribbon rib bones barbecue

Silver tongue lash fluorescent odor

Lush of sap popping broken tree limb

Thank the elegant snarl

For a broken bird's nest

Eggy crest of a wave

Outfoxed airplane swollen vertigo

Go north into the ice go north permafrost
axehandle

Overcomplicated snowshoe mechanism

Movie theater seat fishing, where is it?

Projecting shame tooth twist tie knot

No footprints scribble concrete smoky trashcan

Dance YEEHAW circular around the lunatic
boombox

In the skins of your predators

The flayed carpet of featherless curiosity

Water fountain dry mouth trickster swallow

Not theoretical anymore

You all went cowardly through the gleam

Beaten by Orion's belt I waited outside the temple
of the sparrow

Occasionally lifting my leg on the saintly marble

We have been here before, paperweights for picnic
blankets

Drooling into a wishless fountain of coins

Antarctic diplomas rendered useless

I spit cavities, fillings and stalagmites at you who
went through the painted door

I stayed, bathed in a corduroy swish

Threw my top-hat onto the dewy grass

Smoked out of salad bowls

We dressed in papercuts, carbon

Shredded documents gleefully heated

These things I piled into rubble lungs

And baked into a pie

Blackbird and ground beef zero

Circular, his beergut spills on the table

Planetlike and sebaceous

The accountant's sofas are stuffed with the fur of taxidermized scientists

Galileo blinded by the big picture

Telescopes fear no paradise

Pointing up even as their makers clutch their eyes whimpering

Time evolves depending on velocity simmering on an electric stove

Einstein prove right by a fat man's indigestion

The planet spins vomit vomit vomit

Desires sin as defined by its own judgment

Deep algae bubbles

Holding my nose and hoping

Calculate reason calculate a sickness calculate a cure a trap and a lure

---

If I only had the hands for it

(Remember want does not beget form)

I would construct for you

Such a machine dream of the frozen yogurt dictator

Towering and gorgeous flicker

A shadow spilling across

Where rocks used to make it were yanked from take wallpaper whipcrack flight

Out here in the junkyard with the stonehenged refrigerators

There are no true vegetarians

I am no hunter because the hunter cannot

Put his arrows down on the river-bank safety deposit box

And say no more, speak no symbol crash

Ever polluted, he would starve

Bump no shoulders, crack no boulders

Fry no omelet, he dares not

Rusting in a cornfield

I only have one good dare left in my shirt pocket

Tumbleweed sleep-sickness snowflake exhale

On these walls reptilian snap signal current

I scritch a future with no walls, no hours and no
owls

But sneak in around the back and astrally catch
myself laying the mortar

Satellite grinding the paste circular

Picking up the morning paper from the stoop bent
by the weight of a full gut

Ritual ridiculous

I never want to lose the hunger

So I prepare a gold tipped shovel

You can see the egotistical twinkle from space

But good luck building the necessary kaboom to get
there

I stole all that from the necessary pockets

Circular

Ye blackbirds cackle opening a fresh box of
breakfast cereal

I am no hunter because my arrows are tipped with
marshmallows

It's bigger on the inside

I'm standing outside taco bell

Preparing to go in and order cheap burritos

At the edge of the parking lot

Is a fence

Separating this place

From the amusement park

I can see the rollercoaster periodically rise high above

The screams are highpitched and girlish no matter who is making it

I can see the small kids tugging on their parent's sunblock slathered hands

And the sunburned teenagers pretending to not be scared

They all have tickets in their hands

Having been there a number of times

I know that from inside the park

You can't see out and it seems a lot bigger than it actually is

And I wonder:

Is this the way astronauts feel floating way above the tiny lights of cities at night

As they wait for the right time to eat their tubed astronaut food?

Disemboweled in the shopping mall

All of almost spilled out today

After I handed my inked up job application paper

Filled with references and former employers names
and proof of my citizenship

To the girl behind the starbucks counter

And she said through a mouthful of braces

"We're not hiring right now but I'll give this to the
manager"

Everything nearly spilled out

All the rage which has built up inside me like plaque
on unbrushed teeth

I imagined (And I could see it too, like a drive in
theater just above my nose)

Leaning my head over the tile counter

As if to give her a kiss

And biting her head off in one scissor motion chomp

And saying to one of her shocked coworkers as her spurting headless corpse collapsed on the cash register

"Now I KNOW there's a job opening

Who else do I have to kiss to get it?"

Instead of even saying something witty or mean

I shoved it back down

Like a disemboweled person pushing their intestines back in

To buy more time

All my experience with violence comes from Hollywood

Tom Hanks firing at that german tank with a handgun at the end of saving private ryan

Even in fiction everybody wants to buy more time

And even though my eyesight occasionally tints red

I've never even been in a fight and know no pain beyond my own melodramatics

No pain no gain or maybe just no gain and plenty of pain

Clichés expand popcornish in my lard-streaked imagination

The coffee junkies behind me tapped their feet and scratched their arms waiting for me to move out of the way

I meekly said, "Thank you"

The espresso machine gurgled like a laugh track on an unfunny sitcom

I walked out into the rest of the 2 story shopping mall

Where a poster of a woman in a bra stared at me like a 30 foot tall big brother from a wall

She had the words

HELLO BOMBSHELL

Emblazoned across her chest in red letters

I hear them in my head real sexy over the sound of crashing planes

HELLO BOMBSHELL

And from inside fudruckers I could hear a shamanistic chant proclaiming the bird is the word

A bald man dragged two shrieking mucous leaking children inside with him

One on each hand

And the mothers in public, they pull their children close to them if I walk within ten feet

Like I'm an unmuzzled dog without a metal leash around my finger

A fairy tale monster under the bed only around as reason to keep the kids in school

At the foodcourt the workers pop out like invisible robots to sweep away the trash

And then go back backstage or somewhere where nobody can see them

The hooks in deep kid either be gutted or go to sleep

And you aren't gonna be able to push it out by eating potato chips and playing xbox

When I turned 13 years old

My mother sat me down and told me that now that I was a teenager

I was on my way to becoming a sex crazed immoral monster and how much of a shame it was that I wasn't a girl

And now at the ripe old useless age of 21

I can't look anyone in the eye and I step aside on the sidewalk to let anyone coming walk by

So yeah I'M the monster alright!

I wonder as I watch the plastic Christmas trees twinkle like fishhooks

If I'm alone in this

Or if everyone walks around pretending they aren't disemboweled?

The postal service is letting kids send letters to santa claus in the north pole this year again

And the president is gonna give more money to the banks

So who's propagating a bigger lie?

I hope I am the only lonely person on earth

Because it's nice to have at least one original idea going for you

The strapless plastic watch in my pocket reminds me that I have nowhere I need to go

Without me the wheels will continue to turn but while I'm here there isn't anything left to burn

And while today feels thin and malnourished and the future remains incomprehensible

The past just keeps chewing and slobbering and getting fatter

I sometimes worry that eventually it will catch me in it's flytrap teeth and every day will be yesterday

I hum a warped snatch of a Beatles tune and look at chocolate truffles behind glass display cases longingly

"yesterday all my trouble seemed so far away, now I need to get some decongestant nasal spray"

And yesterday a homeless old person and I crossed the street at the same time

In between the painted white lines that say where it's ok to walk but only when the white flashing sign says when

I couldn't tell what gender he or she was

He or she wore a tattered muddy tarp for a coat
and had dull tarnished eyes like beaten silver

And the edge of the tarp-cape flapped in the
dioxide breeze and touched me briefly on the knee

Giving me a gypsy curse for sure

I could see myself mutating into a hag creature
leering from the dumpsters

HELLO BOMBSHELL

But for now I'm young and broke my wallet has
consumption

And the shopping mall's display windows are
tugging at it's lungs

I'm young and useless except as a bedtime story so
none of the children grow up to be me

Let me remind you that the bird IS the word but I'm
not a bird just sickly and absurd

And I spent six out of my last 20 dollars on cheap
hamburgers and fries

I sucked down their grease and realized I'll never be
close to the best

HELLO BOMBSHELL

All of it nearly spilled out today

But I shoved it back down the way a lazy person like myself will do with a small trashcan full of candy wrappers

HELLO BOMBSHELL

Airplanes are leaving streaks in the sky over the cities like skidmarks on grey underwear

On tables all over the civilized world

The cigarette butts sit cold and lonely in ashtrays until a sexless bony hand picks one up for a feeble fireless drag

And I can hear the sound of chewing

HELLO BOMBSHELL

False starts

Basic survival utensils are worse than propagandists to recognize by the egg whites of their snake eyes

Roll cages sit shiny and unsold on hardware store shelves

"I tell you what"

The second glove is pulled onto the left hand, it makes a snapping noise

"Being an exterminator of clarinets is haaaard work"

Goggles: check

The leopard striped gasmask is hooked up to back mounted laughing gas canisters devoid of mirth

Spacesuit: check

Never fall in love with an astronaut, you'll never touch them on account of the diapers and helmets

Tutu: check, time to slide down the banister

You have no ignition, no inhibitory rhythmic gingersnap on-switch

This isn't the way, even if the secret does cook

Shake the cast iron kitchen stitches

A bakery scent perverts the daisycrushers

Lazing pushers use one arm on the rumble

She asks the righteous question, "Does this pig carcass make my ass look fat?"

No more than the animal gurgling in your young veins m'dear

We've butchered the joke, raised on alfalfa oblivion oldies

Drip drip the little sparrow sips limestoned

Bodily carcrash dream fluid sweetening the deal

A near-hamburger experience, grinding stenographic nerve call centers

Adjusting his tie and eying the cellularly depreciating gavel he intones,

"Your innocent hee-haw is not a matter of pubic onion I mean public opinion heh heh"

There are always gonna be voices shifting their weight to try keep the boat on a steady diet of collision

But I'd rather lick an iceberg and wait for it to sink in revelatory flup

Not that the whales would appreciate my selfless frozen lisp

They understand a way of floating massively graceful bubble

Because the black ops thyroid biblical femur snorters

Only know how to choke, gag coronary heaped

Clicking falsie cleats on the recycled peephole helicopter landing pads

Scratch it halfmoony on the sandstone wall

"I think I sprung a gasket" He clutches his dry yellow rain coat widening blammed

Panoramic mattress stained hand signal

This is the gift of split timeline winesack spelunkings

Crossing the mannequin desert of scarred starbright

"Nothing here but sand man! You promised me RED rocks"

He kicks a cactus, howls and wishes to be back in the dank subway tunnels

Training penciled in shadow answers

We traded time, hours, days, years for echoes down there

They probed my hopeful ragetumors and laughed clankily

Still there are always gonna be ways to dodge that halogen roar

Places to go to when you grow up into something oysterous

I prefer my slime on a lily pad thank you very much, clean up the ol' garbage halo we're going out

We'll take the chicken fingers off the kids menu with nailpolish on the side

And the sleepier kind of hypno conversations until three AM stubbles

As opposed to these sneezing chairsqueaking official sorts of snark

"I've had better hells"

The paranoid mayoral candidate sniffs dismissively to see if the sommelier slipped him a roofie

Or a fizzing eventual meteoric shooting spree headline

Holds me tight nose caught in a morning glory

I don't know anything about any of this except the chuffing opinions on FM radio

Hail the rubber ducky fleet the splash approaches

But what I do know, is you'd shut your ears with glue before you wanted to hear it

A pitchpiped vision of alleyway panthers

Loping from western bellied conspiracy theorist healers

I miss the simple destructive candles of my old religion

But it's not like I can just text message to say I miss them

Technology has no sense of its own technocratic irony

No, this is not the way, you don't negotiate with lynchmobs by offering them inches

There are submarines on patrol even as we whisper under the shimmy of multiplicitous honking gardens

They're only playing at primordialism

I don't care which one I'm talking about but all messiahs require ashes to rise

The ambassadors cower beardless, the people must know, "boxers or briefs?"

If you think I'm being spiritual, watch that crow black triangle morning more closely next time

I may leap into the very maw of the dismembered grandmother clock

But I'll never be bigger than a fine spitshined dust ripple

Gulp that thing quick I'm running out of clever weaponry

I can pass this iridescent lullaby between my teeth and pretend it's all mine

Jet-streaming atomic imitative glow

But I can't thieve the blackberry chin juice stinger

I don't dare bite down into the stiff grenade powdercored sunset apple

Electric wires doused in termite mudmasks

Where-ever you go don't forget your meatcleaver

And whatever you do, don't (and I don't mean this as a typical punchline) don't bite down

A necessity of comas

Unpollinated stopsigns flutter on metal stalks in the lonely western night of great drums

Each moment has starts in another moment, each of equal absurdity

And this moment of ugly slack jawed clarity started unexpectedly

When I went into a public restroom at the same time as a police officer

He was big and muscular, dressed in black with a shiny badge and an oily gun on his hip

He had the swagger of someone who is in control, knows it

And is prepared to defend that control by whatever force necessary

He possessed the same smirk as the young men with tattoos and AK47s he's sworn to arrest

We stood at the urinals and I tried to ignore the specter of authority

I can't piss when I'm nervous and his squawking radio didn't help

He could probably taste my fear oozing out of every sweatgland like some kind of criminal pheromone

I could taste the gulp of it so there's no way a trained fearsniffer could miss it

I washed my hands slowly doing everything I could to ignore him

And as I walked out that thick wooden door into the hallway

I realized that it's always been this way, there's always an us and them or a me and you

A coyote and a roadrunner writhing in technicolor freudian torment

There are those of us who are blunt and polished reactive

Who have the fascist twostep goosestep twelve step swagger

And then there are those of us who sneak around them ratdancing and irrationally guilty

Though we urinate side by side in the same stained porcelain

Some boys have heavier feet to put down

And push their pornographically fickle accelerators

To the euthanasia breakdown blueprint vanishing
point of original sin

They can take a stand on their grandpas' burial
mounds

For hot-rod lust and squealing justice witch burning
ditch digging burden of victory

And for toe tapping bra snapping brutality mentality
of the absolute

But that's not me, my snarl is a lukewarm fictional
sneeze

I'm one of those rare invisible undercooked idealists

Not the kind to wolfwhistle obscenities from
rooftops at passing females

Though sometimes I scorch with a dandelion puffing
wish to partake in the soft zap of their breath

And from my optimist wasteland-tinted glasses
viewpoint in the dust

I know I have an itch of unfinished responsibility
simmering

Scratching out an SOS code in hopefully desiccated crayon gashes

The iron palaces and phallic war-machines of the john waynes and stanley kowalskis

Will wash away in an antiseptic flood from one too many pissing contests

But just to be sure, I can't look over both shoulders at the same time you know

I would like to declare in big neon mercury tainted letters a kilometer high as a kite

An anti-capitalist, anti-communist, anti-terrorist, anti-teaparty,

Anti-hippie, anti-yuppie, anti-democrat, anti republican,

Anti consumerist, anti-psychotic, anti-freeze

Scream at crackable deaf swaying imitative of trees wall of imperial tombstones

Momentary manifesto of flood memoirs

I would like to spit a spite loogey towards the atmosphere and watch it hang there, glistening

I'd like to make a long distance call to hold someone in my arms

I want to sprint up and tell anyone willing to listen for my occasionally gilgamesh heartbeat,

"You and I should lie on the grass with the fruitflies and discarded beer bottles

Watching the stars drift by like pulsing ships that don't know they're already sunk

Give it a try, your bank account can wait

And the tupperware leftovers won't get any more rotten and unedible in your fridge than they are now

I want you to realize and maybe help me convince myself

That even the bent repentant shoeshiners

Can shake off the horseflies, when sharing the soft taste of a stargaze"

Sadly, that kind of talk is nearly a forbidden quantity in this time of illuminated alleyways

We who possess the reinvented double edged silver ego word

Are all too often fed swiftly, finally and drenched in beads of sniper sweat

To convenience stores open all night glowing gasoline high fructose false oasis

Or various snowballing vietnams and their squalling broods

To leaving green lands and parking lots behind for something not too different

Butchering the ideal into palatable chunks, easy to chew

Shoveled into thorazine anti depressant cleaning solution sizzles

To morning pie and black coffee serving diners with angry methmouth waitresses wanting orders

While outside trains and SUVs and greyhound buses obliviously speed through shimmery deserts

To twilight nightlight repetitious existence sustained on foodstamp stews boiled pink

To late night television laughtrack comfortable slip away heart attack bathrobes

To suburban mind sleeping comas, convinced of
their necessity we march on giddy with self
destruction

Tossed into the happymeal furnaces of a plasticized
gaea

A lithe swimmer rising out of pondscum morning
breath is your fantasy now

Consummate volcanic eroticism?

Scheming a tightrope to balance on as it suits my
nausea

The american hallucination will gobble my
innocence with many a fairy tale giant grunt

It stands confident, red white and blown glass
boogeyman outside my bedroom

So I wait out these last few solstices with the blinds
closed to keep out street lights, moonlight

Neighbors fighting, car doors slamming, backfiring
gunshots sirens dog howl serenade

Under the covers with a flashlight and a comicbook

I don't ever want to have what it takes to wear the
big stomping boots

Or slip a silk tie noosey around my neck

For the eventual unknown inevitable whiplash jealous hangman

If I had a time machine I would go skipping forward into the future

And shoot myself dead right when I'll expect it

At least then I'd know when he was coming

I would be my own blue angel countdown timer

But such fantasies are only all too typical as I shake with uncertain mumbled dreamhums

Soothing voice of reasonable conduct intones,

"When you finally stop running stomping pavement flat footed and wheezing the joy of escape

They will suck it out of you drop by drop with the most colorful twisty straws you have ever seen"

Popped stockmarket bubble of chocolate milk children with missing front teeth grim on a carton

Unable to sustain the illusion of rabid seafoam

I lift this clown painted tragedy on my sunburned epiphany for a nickel shoulders

Smiling sly and unwise, a failed cherub with red cheeks

I get down on a bended knee to poke with my tongue

The clear water running scared from well mannered wounds

Svelte impossibility cuts deeper than the blind shine sword of the hypnotist

So as the bluesmen mystics of another century predicted with such bruised wit

Started with something simple as pissing next to a cop in a public bathroom

There will be a reckoning, a beckoning and a crossroads

I can either snicker about my predicament, irreverent and irrelevant

Or I can let the terror-pill of posthumous growing-up dawn upon me bitterly

Honestly though, I'd rather the sound of my
laughter mingles wet with the flushing of waste

Rituals of realization and purification on their way
to vast oceans of chlorine

Future movement

I believe the immense migraine beauty of an iron
plated sadness

It's some scattered papercut intensity, some cirrus
gesture that I can't quite capture

Recognition of a face dozing sudden on my shoulder

Muse of my drooped eyelid flower

I wake folded in sound and mutter that I have the
crash

The one troglodyte unrepentant in his cave-in
soliloquy

Sunflower rattle clutched in my gearshifter hand, oh but I don't have the reach

When it happens I'll send a paper airplane postcard

Tiretracks left out along a squealing asphalt two color kaleidoscope highway

Carbon relic of an age, a moment, a look, a reach

I will squeeze every drop from this ephermal youth

Twisting nails from rotten front porch planks

This is a place built bloodsoaked with a hope of flight

We smelled smoke and decided to consult the bite dried oracle

Locomotives with no passengers but bouncing beds of scrap metal

Whistle greasy lone machine across the planes of a mythic Kansas

Remember the flap of your feet across the suburban almost tombs

The enamel on your teeth was so shiny back then

At the very least we tried to reach for the source of this liquid déjà vu recognition

Tried to push unsuccessfully to convince ourselves of a way to jump the tracks

Only moths understand the ringing of duskpainted clocks

But not us, we have armhairs cold with airconditioning

As you lick that cherry popsicle and some of it runs down the stick onto your sweetened hand

Your hand, my hand, the ambulance crooning

Your hand, my hand somnambulism swooning vultures

Stop to consider as you lift newspaper wings towards flashlight sterilization

Thin like the ribs of anorexic aphrodites splayed formaldehyde in magazine pages

The future, with all its smokestack supermarkets and spires of bacon and gold

All those ed wood film bandit bilingual promises

Already happened

It crashed gasping upon us

A great bleak wave of oil, biscuits, violins and associate degrees

Arthritic heave of an arctic muscle for a chalkmarked finishline

I would race until my lungs crisped but my legs would give out hours before that happened

An eventual skidmark ghost town walk of fame winked star with my name on it

We are the century of the bruise's biggest lie

The plate was licked clean

Flopping cerulean in the mud when it recedes back into stagnation

Not the shade of willow blue I wanted to become

I lit incense and tried to conjure the gentle heat of butterflies

Someone told me there really is a path of smoke

But like I said to the ceiling, only moths understand

So look backwards slick with paranoid bliss

What comes next, like my grin, lacks the jellybean
spark

Because what comes next is polished jade
blindness, an escalation of protoplasm bureaucracy

All engines are moving west now

Cough up the price of a switchblade and have a seat

We only stop to fill up on fluidic melody

All engines point spinning compass panic to the
west

Walls

Whether you actually believe the wall is there

                Across the flattened industrial
gardens of scrap metal flowers and acid-rain
showers

        On the very farthest edges

Doesn't matter

        Because the wall believes in you

        The wall sees you on one side of it

        And feels what may as well be you on the
other side

        Each imagining in the same way

        The wonders on the other side

It grows in a terrible and grey split down the middle
way

What matters is

        If you keep zooming towards it and
bellowing from under a football helmet

At such furious speeds of innocence

You will crash out and the raven-maned machines will pick your pacemaker from the wreckage

Unless of course

There actually isn't

Anything there to smash your faithful hammer into after all

Wouldn't that be awful?